UNDERSTANDING AND HARNESSING THE USE OF iOS17

BEGINNERS GUIDE

NELSON TURNER

TABLE OF CONTENTS

INTRODUCTION

Introducing iOS 17, the latest iteration of Apple's renowned mobile operating system. This highly anticipated update signifies a significant leap forward in elevating the iPhone user experience. iOS 17 has been meticulously designed to address essential aspects of device performance, security, and user satisfaction.

As Apple continues its unwavering commitment to innovation, iOS 17 stands as a testament to the company's dedication to delivering cutting-edge features and robust improvements to millions of iPhone users worldwide. This update introduces a range of new capabilities and enhancements, all aimed at making your iPhone even more powerful, secure, and enjoyable to use.

From temperature management to fortified security, iOS 17 comes packed with features tailored to optimize your day-to-day interactions with your device. Whether you're concerned about issues related to overheating, seeking enhanced security measures, or simply looking for a smoother and more efficient user experience, iOS 17 has you covered.

Join us as we delve into the dynamic landscape of iOS 17, exploring its new features, enhancements, and the profound impact it is set to have on your iPhone experience. With iOS 17, your iPhone transcends being just a device; it becomes a gateway to a world of boundless possibilities and unparalleled convenience.

CHAPTER ONE

GETTING STARTED WITH IOS17

How to Download and Install iOS17

To obtain iOS 17, start by ensuring your data is securely backed up. After that, follow these steps:

1. Open the Settings app on your device.
2. Scroll down and tap on "General."
3. Select "Software Update."
4. You may need to tap "Upgrade to iOS 17" located at the bottom of the screen.
5. Proceed with the "Download and Install" option, or you might be automatically directed to the download and installation process.

Installation Guide Lines Using Beta Public Beta

1. Visit the website beta.apple.com.
2. Sign in using your Apple ID. Note: It's not necessary to use the same Apple ID as your phone, but it can simplify the process.
3. On your iPhone, access the Settings menu, then go to General, and select Software Update.

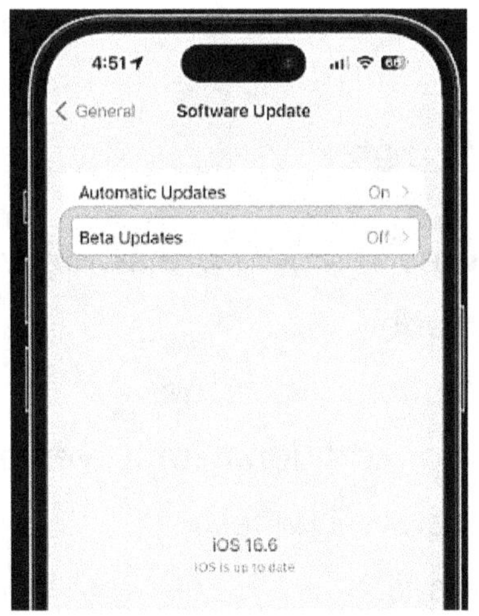

4. Be patient; it might take a moment, but a new option for beta updates will appear just below Automatic Updates.
5. In this menu, you can switch between the options "Off" and "iOS Public Beta."
6. If you used a different Apple ID for the beta program, this is where you can sign in with that secondary ID.
7. Return to the Software Update page, and it will automatically refresh to display any available beta updates.

iOS17 Features

The New features in iOS 17 are as follows:
- StandBy mode
- Enhancements to Messages
- A plethora of additional improvements.
- Contact posters, NameDrop,
- Live Voicemail,
- FaceTime video voicemail,
- A new Siri voice recognition model,
- Huge improvements to autocorrect and dictation, and a lot more.

All these aim to improve the function ability and advancement of the device technology. However, not all the devices or phones that are supporting iOS17

Phones Compatible with iOS17

The availability of features and apps can differ based on your iPhone model, geographical location, language, and mobile carrier. the few listed below are phones that do support iOS 17
- iPhone XR
- iPhone XS
- iPhone XS Max
- iPhone 11
- iPhone 11 Pro
- iPhone 11 Pro Max
- iPhone SE (2nd generation)

Understanding ios17

iOS 17 introduces significant enhancements to Phones, Messages, and FaceTime, providing novel avenues for self-expression in your communication. Moreover, StandBy ushers in a fresh full-screen interface, displaying easily viewable information from a distance when you tilt your iPhone sideways during the charging process.

Updating ios17

1. backup your device

Updates may not always go smoothly, so it's a wise move to back up your phone's data before transitioning to iOS 17. In the event of accidental data loss, you can easily restore it from the backup.

You have the option to back up your phone either to the cloud or to your computer's hard drive. Just ensure that you have sufficient storage available. Apple provides a mere 5 gigabytes of free storage when you sign up for iCloud, and most users store considerably more data on their iPhones. If you require more storage space, you can opt to pay a nominal fee. For instance, 50GB of storage is available for just 99 cents per month.

Ideally, you've configured your phone to back up automatically regularly. This not only simplifies the process when you decide to update the operating system but also acts as a safeguard against losing your cherished photos and other files in case your phone is lost or damaged.

This is also a favorable time to go through your iPhone and remove any unnecessary apps. For example, you might have a space-consuming video game that you haven't played in a while. If you later change your mind, you can always re-download the app.

To check the last backup date for your phone on iCloud, navigate to Settings > your Apple ID > iCloud > iCloud Backup. Once there, you'll have the option to initiate a manual backup by selecting "Back Up Now." Feel free to proceed with that.

2. Go to settings

After ensuring your phone is backed up, follow these steps:

- Tap the Settings icon on your device.

- Navigate to "General."

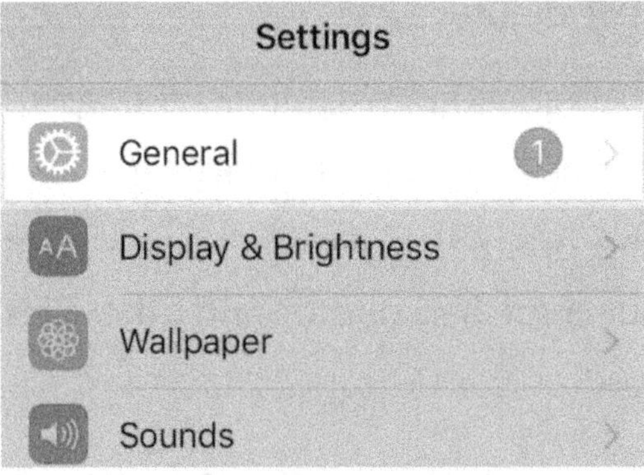

- Select "Software Update," typically the second item from the top.

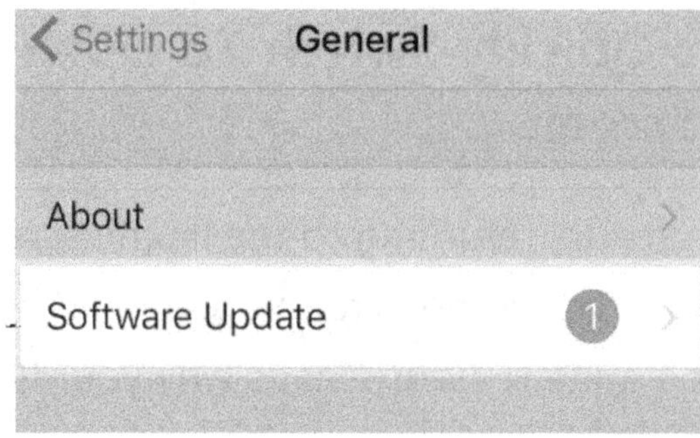

- You may receive a notification that an update is available. If not, click on "Software Update" to initiate a search for updates.
- Proceed to download and install the update. The duration of this process may vary, contingent on the speed of your internet connection, and may take several minutes.

NAVIGATING THE USER INTERFACE

How To Quickly Access Notification Center From The Home Screen

1. Gently tap the area around the screen's border.
2. Swipe your finger downward onto the screen (i.e., perform a downward swipe).

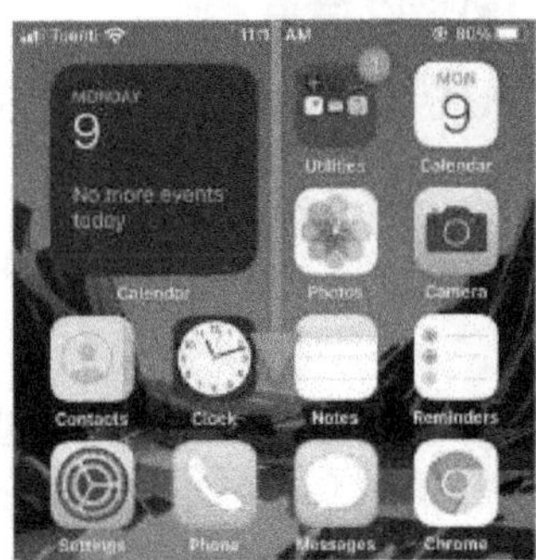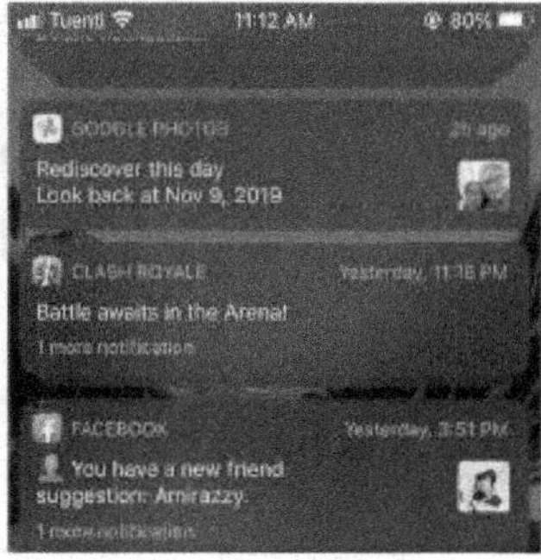

How To Quickly Switch To Open Apps From The Home Screen

Initiating an app, returning to the Home screen, starting another app, returning to the Home screen again, and then reopening the initial app can be quite tedious. That's why your iPhone and iPad provide a more efficient method to switch between recently used apps.

1. Simply double-click the Home button or, for devices compatible with Face ID, gently swipe your finger from the bottom of the device.
2. Swipe through the displayed apps to locate the one you wish to switch to; they are arranged in order of your most recent usage.
3. Tap the app's screen to seamlessly transition to it.

How To Quickly Access Continuity Apps From The Home Screen

Apple allows you to seamlessly transfer your ongoing activity from one device to another, enabling you to pick up right where you left off. For instance, if you're using Safari on your Mac, you can effortlessly switch to your iPhone or iPad and continue browsing.

To initiate this feature:

1. Double-click the Home button or, for Face ID-compatible devices, gently slide your finger from the bottom of the device.
2. Locate and tap the app icon positioned at the bottom left of the screen. (In the absence of an app icon, it indicates that there's currently no suggested app or available handoff app.)

CHAPTER TWO

STANDBY MODE FEATURE

StandBy represents a novel Lock Screen mode introduced in iOS 17, designed to activate when an iPhone is undergoing charging and is placed horizontally on its side. Below is a comprehensive guide to help you begin utilizing this feature.

In iOS 17, StandBy mode is activated by default. However, for confirmation, navigate to Settings -> StandBy and verify that the toggles are in the "on" position.

Next, position your iPhone horizontally on any wireless or MagSafe charger.

Setting Up And Using Standby Mode

StandBy mode is activated by default in iOS 17. However, if you wish to adjust the settings, follow these steps:

1. Navigate to Settings -> StandBy and verify that the toggles are in the "on" position.

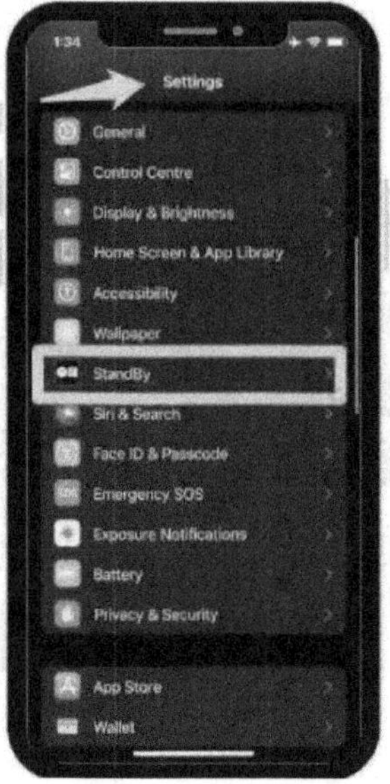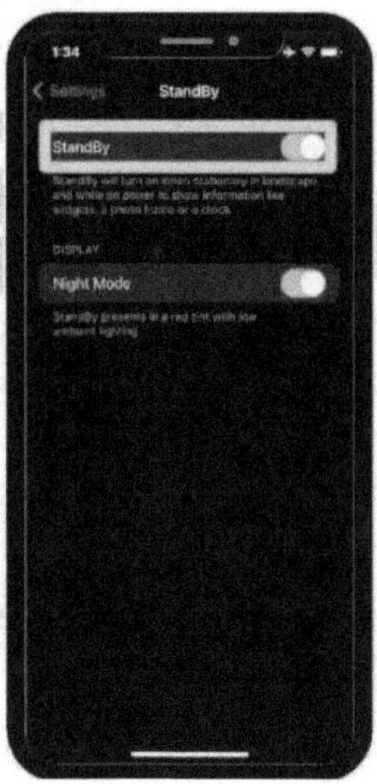

2. To initiate StandBy mode, place your iPhone horizontally on a wireless or MagSafe charger. Alternatively, you can connect your iPhone to a wired charger and position it in Landscape mode. Ensure that your iPhone's display is locked.

3. Once these conditions are met, iOS 17 StandBy mode will activate automatically on your iPhone. The first time you use this exciting feature, you'll be greeted with a welcome screen.

4. Initially, you'll encounter the default StandBy mode, which showcases an analog clock and a calendar widget, providing the

current date and time. This view is fully customizable through the available options, as detailed below.

5. Default StandBy Mode Appearance For the iPhone 14 Pro and 14 Pro Max, which boast an always-on display, StandBy mode remains accessible continuously when your iPhone's screen is off and in landscape mode while charging.

6. For other iPhones compatible with iOS 17, the screen dims after 20 seconds of inactivity. To reactivate the StandBy view, a simple tap on the screen is required.

Customize your standby screen

One of the most captivating and noteworthy additions to iOS 17 is the introduction of the StandBy mode for iPhone. This fresh and innovative feature transforms your iPhone into a smart display when it's positioned horizontally during the charging process. It offers a comprehensive view of the current date, time, incoming calls, Siri responses, and various at-a-glance information, all within a new full-screen interface.

This functionality proves especially handy for your workspace and nightstand. Even when your iPhone is placed at a distance, you can effortlessly obtain weather updates and stay updated on the latest sports scores. In essence, this iOS 17 feature intelligently enhances the capabilities of your iPhone while it's charging and not in active use. This practical tutorial will walk you through the process of activating and utilizing StandBy mode on your iPhones.

StandBy mode offers a range of customization options that allow you to personalize your iPhone's display experience. These features enable you to tailor the appearance and functionality of the StandBy mode to suit your preferences.

Here's a closer look at the ways you can customize StandBy on your iPhone:

Widgets & Photos

With StandBy, you can add various widgets and photos to the display. This means you can choose what information and images you want to see when your iPhone is in StandBy mode. You can select widgets to display weather updates, calendar events, news, and more, making the mode both informative and visually appealing.

How to add widgets to standby mode

- As a default setting, StandBy mode presents the analog clock and calendar widget. To modify this view, you can swipe up on either element. For instance, you have the option to showcase stock information, weather updates, reminders, upcoming events, or even control your HomeKit devices directly from StandBy mode.

- Clock and Calendar Widgets Additionally, you can press and hold either the clock or calendar widget to add or remove StandBy widgets. To remove a widget, simply tap the '-' icon located at the top left of the widget.

- Remove the Widget in StandBy View To add a new widget in its place, select the '+' icon positioned at the top left. From there, you can choose from widget suggestions in the left pane or utilize the search bar to find your preferred widget.
- Choose Widget in StandBy Mode For added convenience, you can create widget stacks, enabling access to multiple widgets with up and down swipes within StandBy mode.

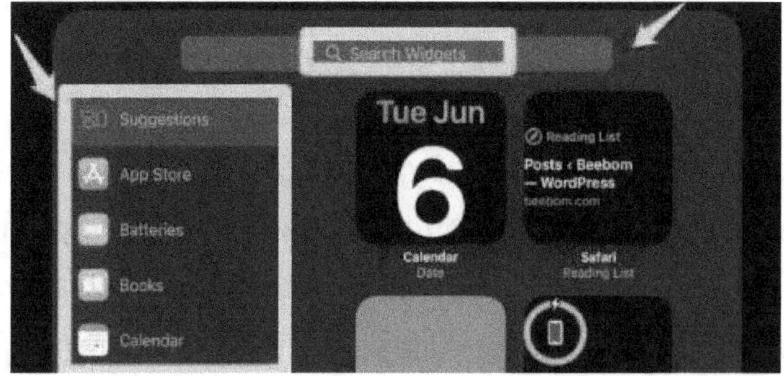

- Moving on, a leftward swipe on the StandBy view reveals all available screens. The initial left swipe presents the Photos StandBy view in iOS 17, which showcases photos and videos from your iPhone's Photos app.

Clock Styles

You have the flexibility to change the clock style in StandBy mode. Whether you prefer a digital or analog clock or want to explore different styles and themes, you can customize the clock to match your taste and needs.

Siri Integration

StandBy fully supports Siri. You can interact with Siri even when your iPhone is in StandBy mode, allowing you to ask questions, set reminders, control smart home devices, and more using voice commands.

Settings up Siri

Setting up Siri on iOS 17 is a straightforward process that allows you to customize Siri to your preferences. Siri is Apple's voice-activated virtual assistant, and it can perform a wide range of tasks on your iPhone. Here's how to set up Siri on iOS 17:

A. **Open Siri Settings:**
   - Start by unlocking your iPhone and going to the home screen.
   - Tap on the "Settings" app, which is typically represented by a gear icon.

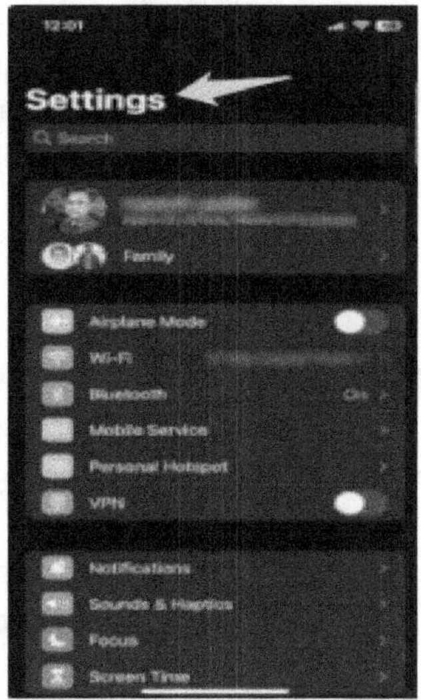

B. **Access Siri & Search:**

- In the Settings menu, scroll down and find "Siri & Search." It's usually listed in the menu below "Privacy."

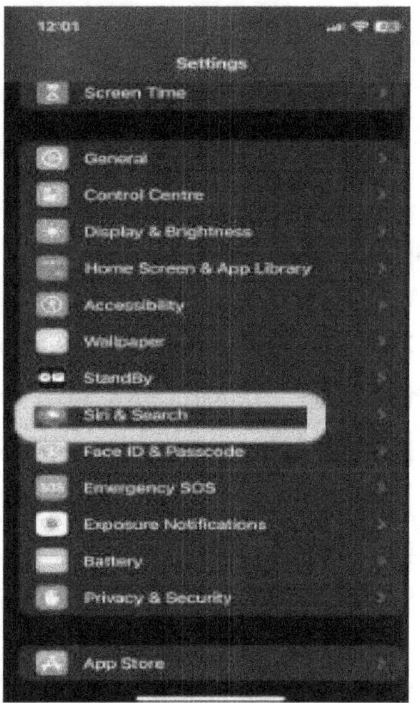

C. **Enable Siri:**

- Select "Listen for," and then pick "Hey Siri" or "Siri" (if available).

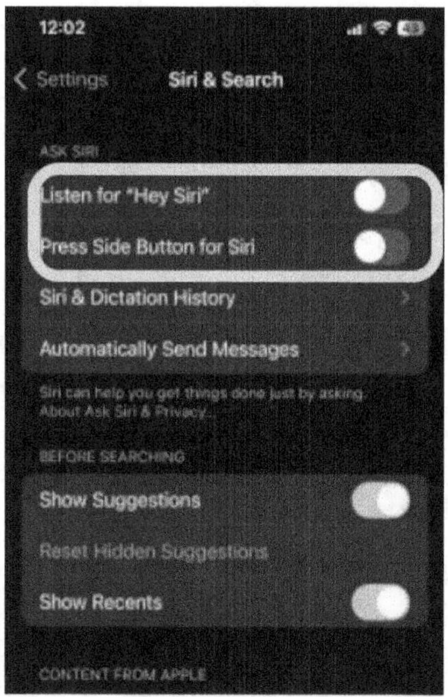

- The tap continues to finish up the settings.

- Please be aware that the choice to use the "Siri" wake word may be available on particular iPhone models in designated languages and regions.

D. **Enable Siri in the Car:**

When discussing the heritage of Apple products, one aspect that often gets overlooked is the integration of CarPlay on iPhones or in general. This oversight may be attributed to its limited use or the fact that not everyone possesses a vehicle or actively utilizes this feature while embarking on journeys. However, in this blog post, we will delve into the world of Apple CarPlay in iOS 17, exploring the new features and the intricacies of its design. So, stay tuned, as we uncover the latest developments!

If you use CarPlay, you can enable or disable Siri in the CarPlay settings section.

To establish a connection between your iPhone and your car, utilize Bluetooth® (consult your car's user guide for specific instructions if necessary).

Features Of Apple Carplay in Ios 17

First, let's explore the novel features of Apple CarPlay in iOS 17 that were previously absent. iOS 17 has introduced a range of enhancements to CarPlay, offering an enriched in-car experience with elements that were previously unavailable. These new features not only extend the functionality of CarPlay but also contribute to a safer and more engaging driving experience. Let's delve into these notable additions:

SharePlay Support: Apple has streamlined the process for users to control their car's music output and utilize mapping features without the necessity of Apple Music or any other Apple-authorized app. You can now make use of SharePlay support to play music from your phone without requiring iTunes, Apple Music, or any specific subscription.

- **Real-time Charging Info for Electric Drivers:** As the number of electric vehicle owners in the country grows, Apple has introduced a helpful feature through Apple Maps. It offers real-time information on the availability of charging stations for electric vehicle drivers, making it easier for them to locate a charging network while on the road. This feature is seamlessly integrated into the Maps app on CarPlay, promising greater convenience, especially as the availability of electric vehicles and charging stations continues to expand.
- **New Interface:** The iOS 17 update for Apple CarPlay brings a fresh interface that's sure to catch your eye. The design overhaul introduces an all-new interface that enhances the ease of replying to messages, ensuring a streamlined and efficient communication experience. Whether you're a passenger or a driver, this interface

simplifies interaction with minimal taps, making it incredibly user-friendly.

Here are some of the key ways to harness the power of CarPlay on your iPhone:

1. App Integration: CarPlay seamlessly integrates with a wide range of apps optimized for in-car use. This includes Apple's applications such as Phone, Messages, Apple Maps, Apple Music, and Siri, as well as third-party apps like Spotify, Waze, WhatsApp, and more. App developers can integrate their apps with CarPlay to provide users with a cohesive and user-friendly experience.

2. Siri Integration: CarPlay offers hands-free control through Siri, Apple's virtual assistant. Users can activate Siri by pressing a button on their car's steering wheel or simply using a voice command. This feature allows users to make calls, send messages, play music, receive directions, and perform various tasks without the need to take their hands off the wheel, promoting safety on the road.

3. Navigation: CarPlay provides an intuitive and familiar mapping experience using Apple Maps. Users can access turn-by-turn directions, search for points of interest, access real-time traffic updates, and receive proactive recommendations based on their calendar, contacts, and previous destinations. Additionally, CarPlay supports third-party navigation apps like Google Maps and Waze for even more flexibility in navigation.

4. Communication: CarPlay enables users to manage their communication effortlessly. You can make and receive calls, send and receive messages, and access your contacts through the integrated Phone and Messages apps. Siri can read incoming messages aloud and allow users to dictate responses, ensuring a safer and hands-free communication experience.

These features make CarPlay a valuable tool for enhancing your driving experience and keeping you connected while minimizing distractions on the road.

To fully utilize these features, ensure you have the latest CarPlay update on iOS 17, and anticipate more exciting enhancements in the coming months of 2023. Apple CarPlay in iOS 17 is evolving to meet the changing needs and preferences of users, enhancing the in-car experience.

- To engage Siri, press and hold the voice command button located on your steering wheel until you hear the distinctive Siri tone, and then proceed to make your voice-activated request.

E. **Finish Setup:**

- Once you've adjusted all the settings according to your preferences, your Siri setup is complete. You can now start using Siri by activating it using voice commands or the designated buttons on your iPhone.

Setting up Siri allows you to access a wide range of features and perform tasks on your iPhone using just your voice. Siri can answer questions, send messages, make calls, set reminders, and much more, making it a valuable tool for hands-free interactions with your device.

Incoming Calls: Incoming calls are seamlessly integrated into StandBy mode. You can see who's calling, answer, and interact with the call without leaving StandBy. This feature enhances the convenience of managing calls when your phone is charging.

Live Activities: StandBy mode accommodates live activities, ensuring that you stay updated on events, appointments, and other real-time information. It's a dynamic way to keep track of your schedule and important notifications

Larger Notifications: Notifications in StandBy mode are designed to be more prominent and easily visible. This ensures that you won't miss important alerts, messages, or updates while your iPhone is in StandBy.

How to customize standby mode

iOS 17 StandBy mode offers a range of customization options that allow you to personalize your iPhone's display experience. These features enable you to tailor the appearance and functionality of the StandBy mode to suit your preferences. Here's a closer look at the ways you can customize StandBy on your iPhone:

How to keep StandBy Mode Always On

For iPhones lacking an Always-On display, StandBy mode will deactivate automatically after a brief idle period. Conversely, if you own an iPhone 14 Pro, 14 Pro Max, iPhone 15 Pro, or 15 Pro Max, you have the option to maintain the iOS 17 StandBy mode continuously. To achieve this, follow these steps:

1. Access the Settings on your iPhone and select StandBy.
2. Within the StandBy settings, tap on Display.
3. Under the "Turn Display Off" section, opt for the "Never" setting.

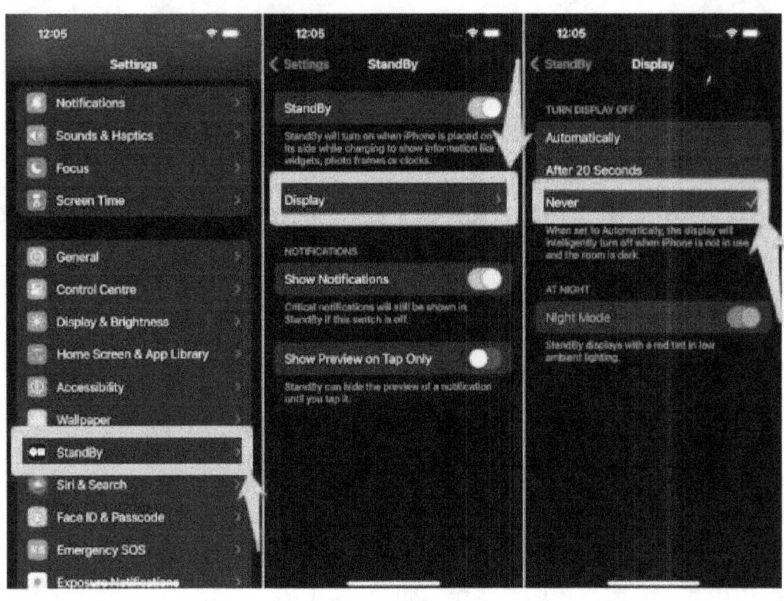

CHAPTER THREE

CUSTOM CONTACT PHOTO FEATURES

Contact Posters provide a means to tailor your representation when making calls. By employing photos and emojis, you can personalize your Contact Poster, which is visible on the recipient's iPhone when you contact them. Similar to the aesthetics of the iPhone Lock Screen, you can pair images with striking typography to make a memorable impact.

However, your Contact Poster extends beyond call screens. It becomes an integral part of your contact details within the Contacts app, ensuring uniformity across various communication and sharing platforms. Apple is also extending this functionality to developers, enabling Contact Posters to be integrated into third-party VoIP apps. As mentioned earlier, customizing your Contact Poster follows a process akin to personalizing your Lock Screen. You have the freedom to select an image, font, and color. The forthcoming steps will illustrate how to accomplish this on devices operating iOS 17.

Note: that the contact poster will also change your Apple ID avatar across Apple Devices.

Enhancing Contact Photo

The iOS 17 update offers an exciting twist for your contacts. Simply navigate to your contacts app, pick the person you want to update and opt for 'Poster' instead of 'Contact Photo.' Discover this fantastic new method to refresh your contacts' appearance and give them a modern makeover.

These features also help you enable and disable the contact poster in case you encounter with annoying contact appearance.

Due to the distinct appearance of Contact Posters, typically centered around one's face, Apple had to relocate the on-screen UI elements that appear during a call. This adjustment also affected the placement of the "End Call" button, causing a bit of an uproar among users.

Personalizing Contact Profiles

Step –by - step guide in customizing contact Photo Features

Certainly, here's an expanded explanation of how to customize your Contact Poster in the Contacts app on your iPhone running iOS 17:

1. **Open Contacts App and Access Your Contact Information:** Launch the Contacts app on your iPhone, and within your list of contacts, tap on your name to access your contact card.

2. **Select the "Contact Photo & Poster" Option:** Within your contact card, look for the "Contact Photo & Poster" option. Tap on it to proceed.

3. **Enter the Customization Mode:** Once in the "Contact Photo & Poster" section, tap the "Edit" button to enable customization. Following this, tap "Customize" to access advanced customization settings.

4. **Choose the "Poster" Option:** Within the customization menu, select the "Poster" option. This is where you will configure your Contact Poster.

5. **Customization Options for Your Contact Poster:**
   - **Select an Image:** Use the buttons at the bottom of the screen to customize your Contact Poster. You can take a new photo using the camera button, choose an existing image from your photo library using the library button, create a personalized Memoji using the Memoji button, or add a simple monogram composed of your initials with the Monogram button.

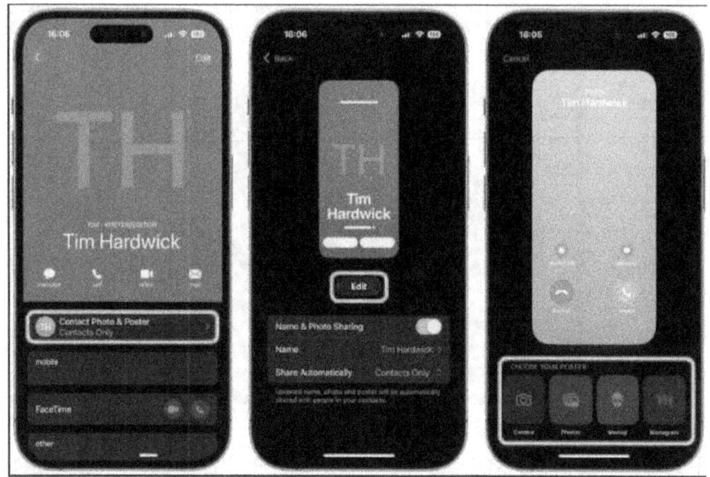

6. **Font and Style Customization:** You can also customize the font size, style, and color to accompany your chosen image. This adds a personal touch to your Contact Poster.

   Please note that this interface doesn't allow you to modify your name; you'd need to change your contact information to do that.

7. **Preview Filters:** Swipe across the Contact Poster to preview a range of filters. These filters include options like black and white, duotone, and color wash in the color of your choice. This enhances the visual appeal of your Contact Poster.

8. **Preview Your Customized Contact Poster:** When you're satisfied with your customization, tap "Done" to preview how your Contact Poster will appear when you call someone. If you're content with the look, tap "Continue."

9. **Further Editing Options:** You have the choice to edit the crop of your Contact Photo, select a different photo, or skip this step entirely at this stage.

By following these steps, you can craft a personalized Contact Poster that not only suits your style but also adds a unique touch to your contact information within the Contacts app on your iOS 17 device.

Now, your Contact Poster and Contact Photo are ready to go. You have the option to automatically share Contact Posters with your contacts, or you can choose to be prompted when sharing with anyone who calls you. This way, your custom imagery remains private until you decide to share it.

Customizing by Changing Contact Posters Photo

There are two methods to set a photo as your Contact Poster. One allows you to promptly capture a selfie using your Camera, and the other lets you choose a photo from your album. Here's how to change the photo in your Contact Poster.

Here are the steps to modify your Contact Poster in the Contacts app:

1. Launch the Contacts app.
2. Locate and select your Contact card from the top of the list.
3. Tap "Contact Photo & Poster."
4. Choose the "Edit" option.
5. To create a new Contact Poster, select "Create New."
6. Under the "Choose Your Poster" section, pick either "Camera" or "Photos" to change the Contact Poster image.

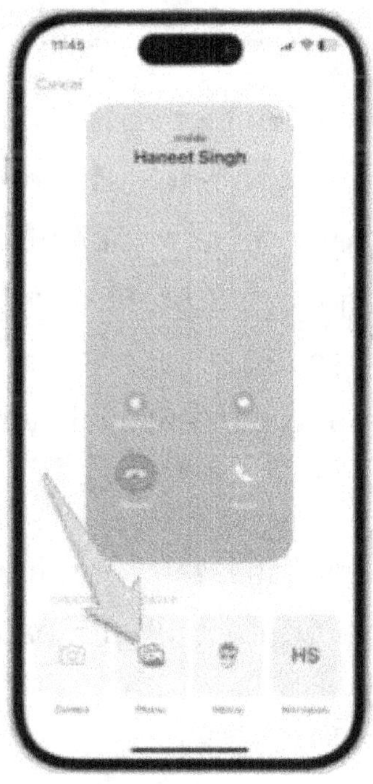

7. You can select any photo from your library and swipe left or right to cycle through various color filters. Some of these filters offer options to adjust the background color, and font, or deactivate any enabled depth effect.

8. To change your Contact Poster's photo:
    - Tap on your name to customize the text's font, size, and color.
    - Use the color circle at the bottom to alter the background color according to your preference. You can also disable the Depth Effect if needed.
    - When you're content with your modifications, select "Done" from the top right corner.

9. On the preview page, tap "Continue."
10. Then, on the Contact Photo page, tap "Continue" to save the changes.

These steps will help you adjust your Contact Poster to your liking within the Contacts app.

Creating a Monogram Text as a Contact Poster

For a more minimalistic approach, you can opt for the Monogram option to create a stylish Contact Poster using text alone. Here's how to craft an eye-catching Contact Poster on your iPhone using Monogram:

1. Open the Contacts app or Phone app.
2. Select your Contact card.

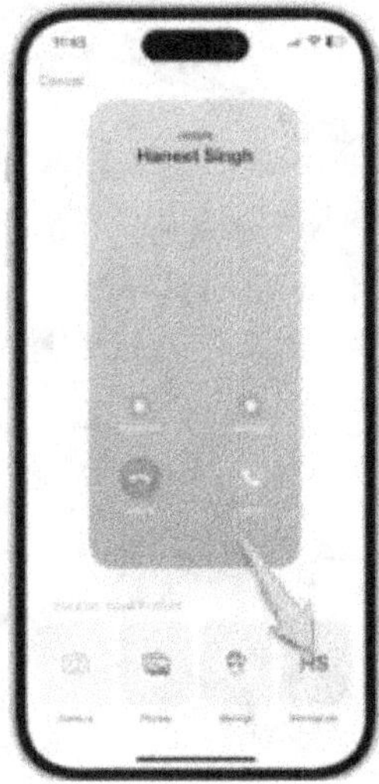

3. Tap "Contact Photo & Poster" and choose "Edit."
4. To create a new Contact Poster, select the "Create Now" option.
5. Choose "Monogram," and you'll see your name with prominent initials in the background.

6. Modify the background color by tapping the color circle located at the bottom left corner.

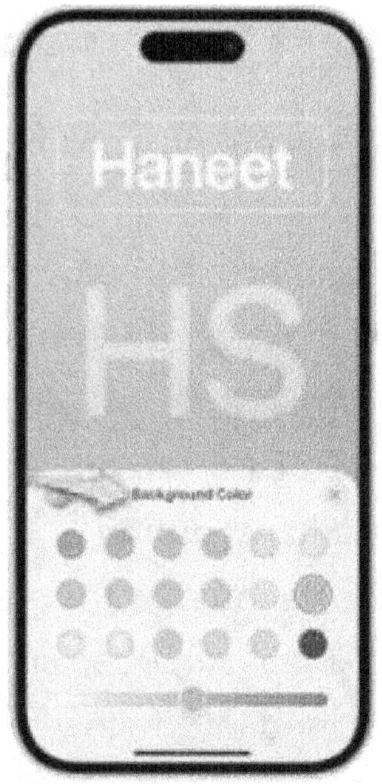

7. If you wish to change the initials, tap the initials icon at the bottom right corner and input one or two characters.

8. To further customize your Monogram, tap the name to adjust the font, size, and color. You can select from four default fonts.

9. Once you're satisfied with your design, tap "Done."

10. On the preview page, tap "Continue."

11. Finally, tap "Continue" on the Contact Photo page to save the changes.

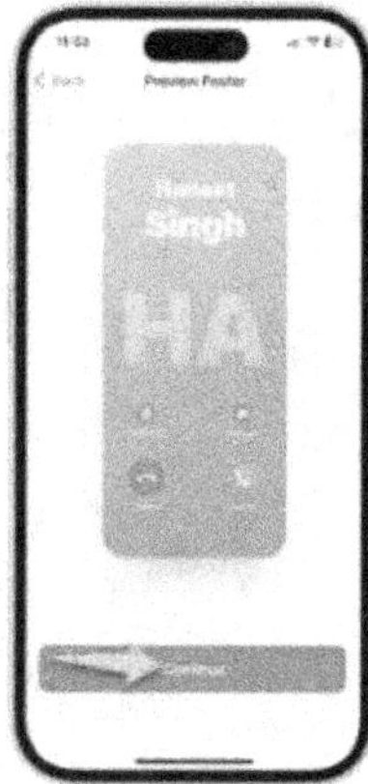

Sharing Contact Posters on your iPhone

Sharing Contact Posters on your iPhone is a simple process. Here's how you can do it:

1. Open the Contacts app on your iPhone.
2. Find the contact whose Contact Poster you want to share and tap on their name.
3. In the contact card, tap on "Contact Photo & Poster."
4. Select the "Share" option.
5. You'll be presented with various sharing methods, such as Messages, Mail, AirDrop, and more. Choose your preferred sharing method and follow the on-screen instructions to send the Contact Poster to your desired recipient.

CHAPTER FOUR

FACETIME NEW FEATURES

A standout feature of iOS 17 is FaceTime Reactions, introducing entertaining 3D effects to your video conversations. You can employ hand gestures to include elements like hearts, confetti, fireworks, and more. These gestures are compatible with the front camera on iPhone 12 and later models.

A FaceTime feature that enables users to share entertaining augmented reality animations during their video calls.

Activating Facetime Reaction

During a FaceTime video call on an iOS 17 iPhone, you can activate on-screen effects such as hearts, balloons, confetti, fireworks, and more. These effects will fill the screen over the FaceTime window.

To activate these overlay screen effects, you can either perform a long press on your image in FaceTime to bring up a reaction options menu, or you can opt for a hands-free approach by triggering the same reactions through physical gestures.

For example, one thumbs up triggers a Like, and two thumbs up are attended by Fireworks. Similarly, one thumb down counts as a dislike, and two thumbs down initiates a rain shower.

To initiate FaceTime on your device, follow these steps:

- Open your device's Settings.
- Scroll down and locate "FaceTime" in the list of settings.

- Tap on "FaceTime" to access its configuration options.
- Toggle the switch to enable FaceTime.

This activates the feature on your device, allowing you to make and receive FaceTime calls.

Below the "You can be reached by FaceTime at" section, you have the option to input your Apple ID or phone number if you haven't done so already. This step is crucial for others to reach you via FaceTime. You can enter either your Apple ID, your phone number, or both, depending on how you want to be reached through FaceTime.

By completing these steps, you'll have FaceTime up and running on your device, and you'll be ready to make and receive video and audio calls with your contacts.

New FaceTime Reactions

Here are eight distinct reactions you can engage in during a FaceTime video call:

1. **Love:** The "Love" reaction is a heartwarming expression of affection and fondness. By selecting this reaction during a video call, you convey deep emotional connection and warmth, making it perfect for sharing love with friends and family.
2. **Like:** The "Like" reaction is a positive sign of approval and agreement. It allows you to quickly indicate that you appreciate or endorse something discussed during the call, offering a straightforward way to express your agreement.
3. **Dislike:** The "Dislike" reaction is a way to communicate disagreement or a negative sentiment regarding a topic or

statement. It provides an option to express your dissent or disapproval when necessary.

4. **Balloons:** The "Balloons" reaction introduces a playful and celebratory element to your video call. It's an excellent choice for adding a sense of joy and festivity to the conversation, especially during special occasions or lighthearted moments.

5. **Stormy Rain:** The "Stormy Rain" reaction brings a dramatic and intense mood to the call. It's suitable for expressing concern or conveying that you're experiencing challenging or emotional circumstances, adding depth to your communication.

6. **Confetti:** The "Confetti" reaction is all about celebrating and adding a touch of exuberance to your video call. It's a symbol of joy and jubilation, ideal for commemorating achievements or happy moments.

7. **Laser Beams:** "Laser Beams" introduce a playful and futuristic vibe to the call. This reaction allows you to have fun and add an element of excitement to your conversation, making it suitable for more energetic interactions.

8. **Fireworks:** The "Fireworks" reaction signifies grandeur and enthusiasm. By using this reaction, you create an atmosphere of celebration and delight, making it perfect for marking significant milestones and cheerful gatherings.

These reactions are crafted to enrich your communication, offering diverse means to convey emotions and thoughts during a video call. They facilitate a more nuanced and captivating exchange with your fellow call participants.

How to turn on Live Voicemail in iOS 17

Enabling Live Voicemail in iOS 17 is a straightforward process, as it's typically activated by default. However, you have the option to turn it on or off based on your preference.

1. Begin by opening the settings on your iOS device.
2. Scroll down the menu and locate the Phone app.
3. In the fourth section, you'll find Live Voicemail. Here, you can easily toggle the switch to activate or deactivate it as desired.

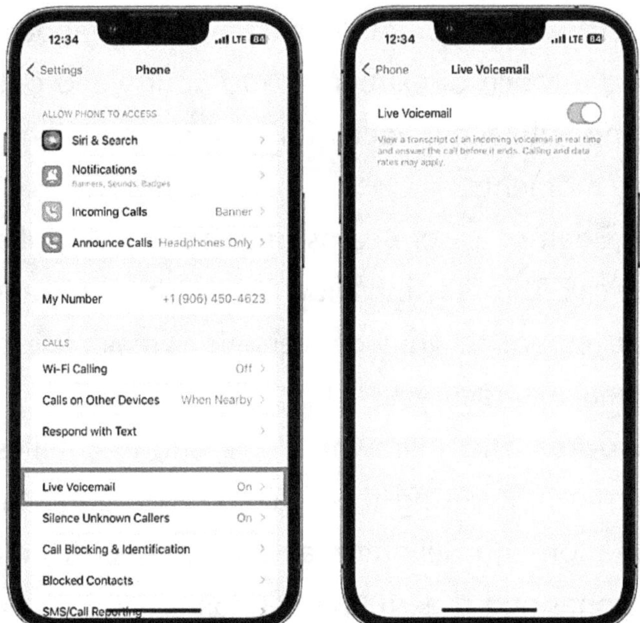

Once Live Voicemail is activated, your iPhone will provide a live transcription of spoken words during incoming calls. This feature also offers on-screen buttons for answering calls while the caller is leaving a message.

From our initial usage, Live Voicemail has proven to be a seamless and user-friendly experience. However, it's important to note that there may be a brief delay before the caller's words appear on the screen. In some instances, the caller might hang up before you have the chance to read their message, potentially expressing their impatience for not answering the call.

Instructions for Capturing a FaceTime Video or Audio Message

When you initiate a FaceTime call and the recipient can't answer, you have the choice to leave either a video or an audio message, depending on the type of call you made. If you're making a FaceTime video call, you can record a video message, while an audio message can be left if it's a FaceTime audio call.

To leave a message, simply initiate a FaceTime call as you normally would. After the call goes unanswered, you'll find an option labeled "Record Video," enabling you to create your message. Once your video message is recorded, you'll be presented with a preview and the option to re-record it if needed.

Here's how the process of leaving a FaceTime message functions on devices running iOS 17, using a missed video call as an example.

1. Within the FaceTime application, select a contact from your list for a video call.
2. If the call goes unanswered, tap the "Record Video" option.
3. To record your message, tap the "Record" button, and when you've finished, tap the "Stop" button.
4. You can then view the recorded message by tapping "Play."
5. If you're satisfied with it, press the "Send" button; otherwise, select "Cancel."

Using FaceTime controls

During a FaceTime call, you can utilize the FaceTime controls to enable or disable your speaker, camera, and microphone, capture a Live Photo, and perform additional functions. If the controls are not visible, simply tap your screen to reveal them.

When engaged in a FaceTime call, the FaceTime controls provide you with various options for managing your call experience:

Speaker Control: You can switch between using the built-in earpiece or the device's speaker. This is useful when you want to share the call audio with others in the room or prefer a hands-free conversation.

Camera Control: You can toggle your camera on and off. Turning off your camera means your video feed won't be transmitted to the other person, effectively switching to an audio-only call.

Microphone Control: You can mute or unmute your microphone, which allows you to control whether the other person can hear your voice. This is handy if you need a moment of silence or privacy during the call.

Live Photo: If you want to capture a special moment during the call, you can use the Live Photo feature to take a photo. Live Photos capture a short video clip along with the image, providing a dynamic memory of the call.

Additional Functions: Besides the mentioned controls, FaceTime provides additional functions such as switching between the front and rear cameras, adjusting the call's volume, and more, depending on your device and software version.

In case the controls aren't visible from the start, there's no need to be concerned. Just tap your screen, and the controls will appear, granting you swift access to these features, thus enhancing your ability to customize your FaceTime call and improve your overall calling experience.

Sharing your screen in a FaceTime call

1. During a call in the FaceTime app on your iPhone, tap the screen to show the FaceTime controls (if they aren't visible), then tap the Share Content button.
2. To share your whole screen, tap Share My Screen.
3. A countdown from 3 to 1 appears on the Share Content button, and then a small image of your screen appears in the FaceTime call. The others on the call can tap it to enlarge it and view your content.

To stop sharing your screen, tap the Share Content button.

CHAPTER FIVE

MASSAGES UPGRADES

The iPhone's Messages app, often referred to as "iMessage," has received several enhancements. These include a redesigned tools menu for centralized access to all your iMessage apps, audio message transcription, and an enhanced search filter to facilitate the discovery of specific content within previous message conversations.

The new iMessage app menu accompanies a host of fresh features, including message stickers, enhanced search filters, the Check-In safety feature, and more. These enhancements are part of Apple's ongoing endeavors to "elevate the user communication experience" on the iPhone in iOS 17.

Apple's Messages app underwent a significant transformation with the introduction of an expandable menu for iMessage apps on the iPhone. This update ushers in a cleaner and more user-friendly user interface. Initially, you might wonder, "Where have the iMessage apps gone in iOS 17?" Let's explore how to locate, incorporate, and tailor these apps.

Apple describes the new user interface as follows: "An expandable menu, easily accessible with a tap, has been introduced to showcase iMessage apps, giving Messages a more streamlined appearance."

Where Can You Find iMessage Apps in iOS 17?

To access your iMessage apps in iOS 17, follow these steps:
   1. Launch the Messages app on your iPhone running iOS 17.

2. Instead of the apps appearing above the keyboard, tap the "+" icon located to the left of the text field.

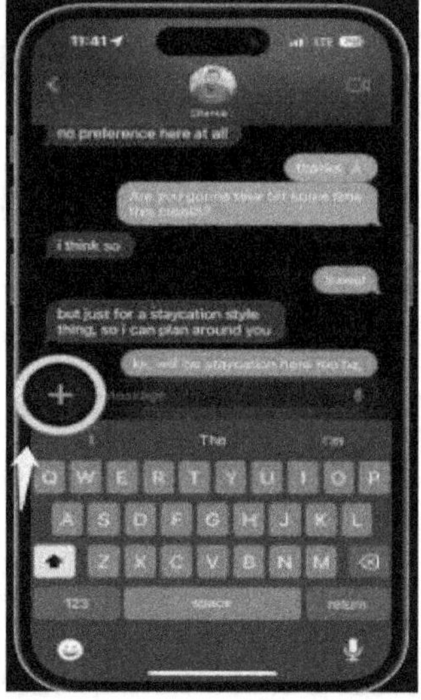

3. Initially, you will see the primary six native apps.

4. To view the additional iMessage apps, simply swipe up or tap the "More" button.

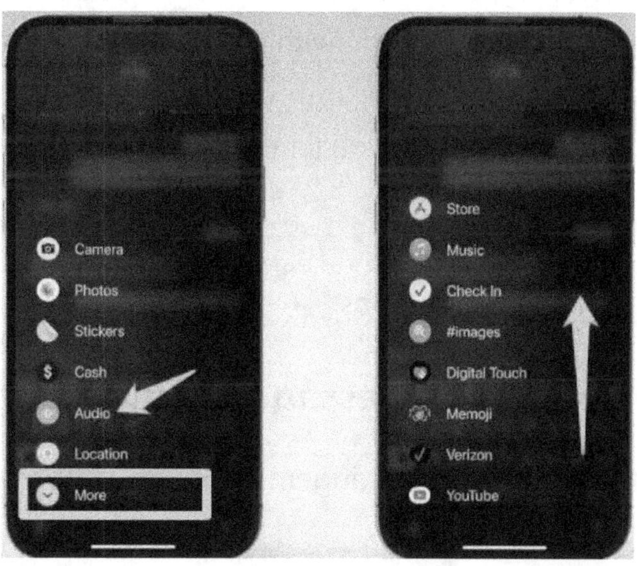

5. Note that leaving voice messages in the Messages app can now be found under "Audio" in the app menu.

6. For a quick way to open Photos, perform a long press on the "+" icon.

Incorporating and personalize iMessage apps

To add and customize iMessage apps in iOS 17, here are the procedures to be taken:

1. Press and hold iMessage apps to rearrange them as you desire. You have the flexibility to move them from the lower section to the top section, allowing you to prioritize your most frequently used apps.
2. To add new apps, simply tap "More," and from there, select "Store" to incorporate new iMessage apps.
   - However, please note that, as of now, the "Store" cannot be relocated from the lower section to the top section, or elsewhere.
3. Currently, there doesn't appear to be a built-in method to delete apps directly from within the Messages app. Hopefully, such functionality will be introduced in the future. For now, to manage and delete apps, you'll need to navigate to
   - "Settings" >
   - "Messages" >
   - "iMessage Apps."

Consolidated iMessage Applications

To personalize the arrangement of your apps in Messages, follow these steps:

1. Launch the Messages app and open any active conversation.
2. Locate and tap the plus icon situated in the lower left corner of the screen.

3. Find the app you wish to reposition.
4. Press and hold on to the app.
5. Drag the app to the desired location on the list.
6. Release the app to confirm its placement.

Exploring iOS 17 Security: Ultimate Protection for Your iPhone

Discover the cutting-edge security measures designed to protect your valuable data and provide you with unparalleled peace of mind for your iPhone. In this guide, we delve into advanced security features, such as robust encryption, biometric authentication options, and enhanced defense against malware and cyber threats.

Stay with us as we unveil the comprehensive security provisions of iOS 17, ensuring that your iPhone remains a fortress of protection!

Join us for an informative journey that covers these incredible features in just ten minutes. In this brief span, we'll explore a plethora of features that will revolutionize your daily mobile experience. Dive into the capabilities of iOS 17, which include intuitive multitasking, advanced privacy settings, revamped notifications, and much more.

Our concise explanations and practical demonstrations related to the new features in iOS 17 ensure that you can seamlessly integrate them into your digital routine.

Whether you're an avid Apple enthusiast, a tech connoisseur, or simply curious about the latest iOS 17 updates, this video is the perfect resource for you.

Safety And Convenience Feature

Make sure you don't pass up the chance to experience the incredible new features however, the subject mater will not going to be analyzed here.

Below, are some features of iOS 17:

1. Receive Sensitive Content Warnings
2. Enable Private Browsing in Safari
3. Automatically Manage Verification Codes Cleanup
4. Utilize Interactive Widgets on Your iPhone
5. Create a Personalized Voice on Your iPhone (For New Phone)
6. Accessing Previous Day's Weather Updates
7. Activate Accessibility Features via Spotlight Search
8. Controlling Focus Modes Silently
9. Utilizing Text Magnification
10. Autofill Verification Codes Received via Email
11. Sharing Passwords with Trusted Contacts

Navigating Conversations With Ease

How to use the new Messages features in iOS 17

In this guide, we'll explore the new capabilities and improvements in Messages made possible by iOS 17. You'll discover several new features that can enhance your messaging experience, along with enhancements and reorganization of some existing features such as:

Check-in

With the Check-In feature in iOS 17, you can share your estimated time of arrival with a trusted contact and set up an alert if you deviate from your expected arrival time.

Here's how to use it:

- In a conversation, tap the + (plus) button located next to the text input box.
- From the list of options, select "Check In."

- Tap "Edit" to customize your Check-In. You have two options to choose from:
    - ✓ "When I arrive": You can specify a destination, mode of transport, and an estimated travel time. If you don't reach your destination within the estimated time, the app will check in with you.
    - ✓ "After a timer": Select the desired timer duration, and the check-in will occur once that chosen period has passed.

The Check-In feature is a straightforward way to ensure your well-being. If you don't respond to the Check-In prompt within 15 minutes, your chat contact receives a message alerting them that something might be amiss. This alert is also triggered if your phone has been offline for an extended period.

In addition to the alert, your trusted contact receives essential information, including your last known location, as well as details about your phone's battery and cellular signal strength (including your Apple Watch, if you have one). You have the option to adjust the level of information shared when configuring the Check-In feature.

If you select the "When I arrive" Check option and you reach your designated destination within the specified time, there is no prompt at your end. Instead, the person you're communicating with receives a notification confirming your safe arrival.

Audio Massage Transcriber

The new automatic transcription feature in iOS 17 provides a helpful alternative for those who are unable to listen to audio messages or prefer to read the content.

When you receive a voice message, it will include an automatic text transcription below it. This allows you to quickly grasp the message's content without the need to press play. It's important to note that this feature is always enabled, and there is no option to disable it.

Searching With Multiple Filters

In iOS 17, you can combine multiple terms and filters within a single search in Messages. Here's how to do it:

- In the main conversation list, drag it down to reveal the search box at the top.
- Start your search by typing something, such as a person's name or a keyword.

- As you select a filter from the drop-down suggestion list, you can add additional filters.

For instance, you can search for links that contain a specific word or locate photos sent by a particular contact, all within a single search query. This streamlines the search process by allowing you to use multiple criteria simultaneously rather than conducting separate searches for each.

Navigation and replies

In iOS 17, you may have encountered situations where you left a group chat and returned to discover a backlog of messages. To address this, there's a new feature: a small arrow on the right-hand side that allows you to easily return to the point in the conversation where you last left off. This makes it convenient to catch up on what you've missed, and it applies to both one-on-one chats and group conversations.
Additionally, iOS 17 introduces an improved method for replying to messages. You can now swipe to the right on a message to initiate a quick reply. This streamlined approach simplifies the process of responding to messages.

Location sharing

The iOS 17 update brings enhancements to location sharing, making it more convenient. You can now share your current location in real-time directly from the Messages app, eliminating the need to switch to Apple Maps or the Find My app.
Here's how to do it:

- In a conversation, tap the + (plus) button located to the left of the text input box.
- Select "Location" from the list of options.
- By default, your location will be shared in real-time. Tap "Share" and then choose from options like "Indefinitely," "Until End of Day,"

or "For One Hour" to specify how long you want to share your location.

- Alternatively, you can tap the pin icon on the left and then select "Send Pin" to share your current location without real-time updates.

Whichever location-sharing option you choose, will appear as an embedded message within the conversation. You can also access options to request the other person's location or stop sharing your location by tapping on their name at the top of the conversation.

Enable automatic deletion of verification codes

If you've implemented two-step verification for your crucial accounts, you may receive verification codes via text messages on your iPhone to authenticate your identity when logging in. For added security and to maintain a clean conversation list, Messages can automatically remove these verification codes once they are no longer needed. To set this up, access your iOS settings, scroll to the section dedicated to built-in apps (located below App Store and Wallet & Apple Pay), select "Passwords," go to "Password Options," and activate the "Clean Up Automatically" feature.

Precision Search

Utilize the Find My app on your device such as iPhone 15 and iPhone 15 Pro models to rendezvous with a friend.

Please note that Precision Finding for People is accessible in specific countries and regions, and both you and your friend must be using an iPhone 15 or iPhone 15 Pro model to take advantage of this feature.

If you're using a different iPhone model to locate someone, refer to the "Locate a friend" section.

1. Launch the Find My app on your iPhone.

2. Tap "People" at the bottom of the screen, then select the name of the friend you wish to meet.

3. If you and your friend aren't already sharing locations, you might need to either share your location with them or request their location.

4. Choose one of the following options:
    - To view your friend's location on a map: If you're not near, tap "Directions" to get closer to their location.
    - To locate your friend nearby: If you're in the vicinity, tap "Find" to notify your friend that you're attempting to locate them, then follow the onscreen instructions to get directions to their location.

5. As you approach each other, an arrow will indicate the direction to your friend along with an estimate of their distance. The screen will turn green when you're heading in the right direction.

6. Once you've successfully located your friend, tap the "Close" button.

7. In case you receive a notification that a friend is trying to locate you, you can tap "Share" to facilitate their arrival. If you've already shared your location with them, they will see your position relative to theirs. (You can cease sharing your location at any time.)

Revamped Location Sharing

Using your iPhone, you have the option to share your location with family and friends. This allows you to stay connected, plan around events, and be informed when a family member reaches home. You can share your location through various apps and have the flexibility to select which specific location details you'd like to share.

Share Your Present Location One Time

You can send a snapshot of your current location. The recipient will only see that specific location and won't be able to track your movements.

Open a conversation or begin a new message. Tap the Plus button (+), then select Location. Tap the Map Pin button, choose Send Pin, and send your message. In iOS 17 or earlier, you can share your current location in Messages by tapping the person's name at the top of the conversation and selecting "Send My Current Location."
You can also share your current location by dropping a pin in Maps.

When You Share Your Location On The Way To A Destination

- When you share your ETA in Maps, you provide your Live Location, allowing the recipient to track your real-time movements.
- During a Check-In session, if your iPhone doesn't reach the expected destination, Check-In alerts your trusted contact. It shares your current location, network signal strength, battery status, and possibly your route.
- After ending a Check-In session, the shared location persists briefly, but it only includes the last known shared location, not your ongoing movements.

Share your current location continuously in real-time

You can share your Live Location in either "Find My" or "Messages", allowing friends and family to track your real-time location, including your direction and speed. Regardless of the app you use, the sharing process remains the same.

To begin sharing your ongoing location using Find My

1. Open the Find My app.
2. Go to the "Me" tab and enable "Share My Location."
3. Navigate to the "People" tab and tap the "Add" button.
4. Select "Share My Location" to add a friend and initiate location sharing.
5. If you're part of a Family Group, your family members will already be listed.
6. Choose the duration for location sharing, whether for an hour, until the end of the day, or indefinitely.

To Initiate Sharing Your Ongoing Location Using Massages

1. Tap the Plus button within your conversation to share your Live Location directly in the chat.
2. The recipients in that conversation can tap your location message to view your position on a map and obtain directions to your ongoing location.
3. Alternatively, tap the name of the individual or group at the top of the conversation.
4. Then, tap "Share My Location" (or select "Request Location" if you want them to share their location with you).

5. Opt for the duration you wish to share your location: for an hour, until the end of the day, or indefinitely.

What Happens When You Share Your Ongoing Location

The individuals you've shared your location with have the following capabilities:

1. Find your Live Location through various means, such as Find My, Maps, your contact card in Contacts, or by tapping your name at the top of a Messages conversation.
2. In a Messages conversation, they can view your general location beneath your name and access your Live Location by selecting your name. When sharing location in a group chat, everyone in the group can see your whereabouts.
3. Receive directions to your location via Maps.
4. Establish notifications for your arrivals or departures from specific locations.

If they set up a location-based notification, you will receive a corresponding notification. In the case of recurring notifications, such as being alerted every time you leave work, you need to accept the invitation first.

Additionally, while sharing your ongoing location, you can also:

- Share your location via satellite in areas lacking Wi-Fi or cellular coverage.
- Utilize Precision Finding for pinpoint location accuracy when both you and the person you're sharing with have an iPhone 15 or iPhone 15 Pro.

Cease Location Sharing With A Specific Individual

When you decide to cease sharing your location with someone in one application, your location sharing is universally discontinued across all applications. This discontinuation does not trigger a notification to the person from whom you're revoking sharing.

Here are the steps to stop sharing your location in different apps:

For Find My:
1. Access the People tab.
2. Select the person you wish to stop sharing your location with.
3. Scroll down and tap "Stop Sharing My Location."

For Messages:
1. Open the conversation with the individual or group you've shared your location with.
2. Tap the name of the person or group located at the top of the conversation.
3. Tap "Stop Sharing."

For Maps:
1. Tap "Sharing with..." found at the bottom of the screen.
2. Choose the name of the person with whom you want to discontinue location sharing.

Cease Location Sharing With All Contacts Momentarily
1. Open Find My.
2. Navigate to the "Me" tab.
3. Disable "Share My Location."

If you choose to reactivate "Share My Location," those you've shared with before will regain access to your location information.

Transcribe Audio Massages

Utilizing Audio Message Transcriptions in iOS 17 is straightforward. These transcriptions are automatically activated once you've updated to iOS 17. After sending an audio message, the transcript will be displayed below the audio bars. Note that in the case of longer audio messages, the transcript may be truncated.

Apple debuted audio messages with the launch of iOS 8 back in 2014. These audio messages, distinct from voicemail, involve sending short audio recordings within Messages, and they've gained popularity as a means of communication.

Although dictating a message might seem more convenient than typing it, audio messages do come with the requirement that the recipient be in a quiet environment to listen to them. Additionally, unless the recipient is using headphones or earbuds, audio messages can be heard by those in proximity.

iOS 17's transcription feature allows you to read your audio messages rather than listen to them, providing a potential solution to these challenges. However, the key question is, how effective is this feature in practice?

How To Utilize Audio Message Transcriptions

Using Audio Message Transcriptions
Audio message transcriptions are activated automatically once you've installed iOS 17. After sending an audio message, the transcript will display below the audio bars.

For longer audio messages, the transcript might be truncated. In such cases, you can tap an arrow to access a new screen with the complete transcript.

In iOS 17, when a person sends you a voice message, it comes with an accompanying text transcription displayed below it. This transcription allows you to read the message's content without needing to play the audio. It's a convenient feature, especially when you prefer reading the message or if you're in a situation where playing the audio isn't feasible.

The text transcription is permanently attached to the voice message, meaning you cannot disable this feature. Therefore, it automatically transcribes the content of any voice message you receive, enhancing the accessibility and usability of voice messages for a broader range of users. This feature is particularly valuable for individuals who may have difficulty hearing or prefer reading messages rather than listening to them.

Findings from Evaluating Audio Message Transcriptions

Loud music, such as the group Outkast playing in the background, might not appear to impact the accuracy of audio message transcripts. The messages were transcribed without any issues, even with the music, and none of the lyrics were included in the transcription. I can't vouch for extremely noisy environments like concerts, but typical everyday noise levels didn't seem to significantly affect the accuracy of the transcriptions.

Interestingly audio messages e.g. in Spanish can be transcribed if your iPhone's language is set to English. When I set my iPhone's language to Spanish and sent an audio message in Spanish, there was no transcription. The same occurred when I attempted to send a message in English while my iPhone was set to Spanish. I conducted a similar test with German and obtained comparable results.

Audio message transcriptions generally provide a decent understanding of your messages, but there is room for improvement in this feature. Your iPhone may struggle with proper nouns, and speaking rapidly could result in words being transformed or combined in unusual ways. It's possible that individuals with accents or those who don't speak English as their primary language may face challenges with transcription accuracy. Additionally, this feature was only functional when my iPhone was set to English, and it would be beneficial for Apple to extend this feature to other languages.

If you encounter issues with transcriptions, speaking slowly and enunciating each letter can help improve your iPhone's accuracy in transcribing your messages.

Key Information:

- Audio messages in the Messages app are now automatically transcribed.
- Transcriptions are conveniently located beneath each audio message for easy reading and reference.
- By default, audio message transcriptions are automatically generated for all received audio messages upon delivery.
- The quality and accuracy of the transcriptions may vary based on factors such as audio message quality, language, accent, and other variables.

Furthermore, audio messages received in the Messages app are now transcribed, providing the convenience of reading rather than immediate listening. This feature simplifies staying updated with your audio messages in various situations. Let's explore this feature and its benefits for managing audio messages seamlessly.

Benefits of Audio Message Transcriptions

1. Enhanced Privacy: Audio messages no longer require being played audibly, allowing for privacy in public or formal settings.
2. Accessibility: Transcriptions are conveniently located beneath each audio message, facilitating easy comprehension.
3. User-Friendly: The feature is automatically enabled, eliminating the need for manual activation.
4. Improved Productivity: Users can efficiently review and respond to messages via transcriptions, bypassing the need to listen to the complete audio.

CHAPTER SIX

AIRDROP IMPROVEMENTS

AirDrop enables the wireless transfer of photos, videos, web content, locations, and various files to nearby devices and Mac computers. It leverages Wi-Fi and Bluetooth® for data transmission, requiring both to be active. To utilize AirDrop, you must be logged in with your Apple ID. All transfers are encrypted to ensure security.

These improvement brings about significant changes regarding NameDrop, proximal sharing, and internet file transfers are now possible. Furthermore, a new SharePlay feature enables shared media experiences.

Mastering the effective use of these airdrop features.

Extended Connectivity

1. NameDrop

NameDrop is an innovative AirDrop capability created to streamline the sharing of contact details between two iPhones. As you bring two devices in proximity, an automatic contact-sharing interface will pop up.

- **Tap to Share**: With a simple tap on the popup, you can access the contact information and Contact Poster of the person you're sharing with. You can opt to either select "Receive Only" or share your contact details in response.
- **Custom Sharing:** You have the flexibility to pick which phone number and email address you'd like to share. If the recipient is

already in your Contacts app, their information will be updated accordingly.

- **Compatibility:** NameDrop seamlessly functions between two iPhones running iOS 17.

2. Proximity Sharing:

This happens by simplifying the process of sharing files or photos with someone in close physical proximity.

Here are the steps for sharing files or photos using NameDrop:

- Choose the File: Pick the file or photo you want to share.
- Proximity Sharing: When both your unlocked iPhone and the recipient's unlocked iPhone are close, the sharing interface will appear automatically, eliminating the need to access the Share Sheet.
- Simple Sharing: Just tap the Share option that appears to send the content to a nearby person. No additional permissions are required, making the transfer hassle-free.
- Configure Settings: You can control proximity sharing by going to Settings > General > AirDrop and toggling "Bringing Devices Together" on or off.

CHAPTER SEVEN

KEYBOARD ENHANCEMENTS

iOS 17 for iPhone introduces multiple keyboard enhancements, streamlining typing, message organization, and navigation for a more intuitive and user-friendly experience.

It brings a host of updates to your iPhone, some of which may not have received as much attention as the high-profile features. These updates include keyboard improvements, which, while considered minor tweaks, can significantly impact your iPhone experience, depending on how you use them.

Autocorrect – an Intelligent assistant

In iOS 17, Apple is enhancing text input systems on the iPhone. This includes improvements to autocorrect with the integration of AI to reduce typos, as well as enhancements in what Apple refers to as "intelligent input." Additionally, Dictation is receiving improvements for more accurate voice recognition. I've tested these changes in the initial iOS 17 beta to assess their effectiveness, and here are my findings so far.

Enhancing iPhone Text Input with AI for Smarter Typing

How can I enhance typing precision on my iPhone? Here are the tips and techniques for quicker and more precise typing on your device:

1. Activate auto-correction and predictive text.
2. Employ text replacement shortcuts.
3. Become proficient with the QuickPath keyboard.
4. Easily capitalize words.
5. Enable the one-handed keyboard for convenience.
6. Customize your keyboard settings.

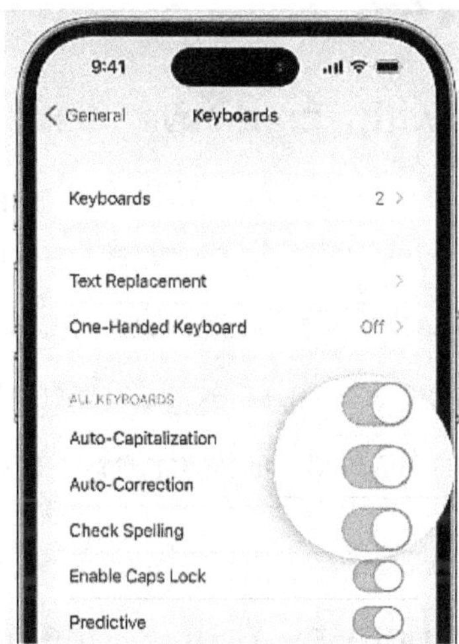

7. Harness the power of voice dictation.
8. Enable haptic feedback for tactile response.

Autocorrect Advancements in iOS 17

In iOS 17, Autocorrect has undergone a significant update, leveraging a cutting-edge on-device machine-learning language model to enhance word prediction. Although Apple refers to this technology as "machine learning," it essentially incorporates artificial intelligence (AI) to take Autocorrect to the next level.

While the core function of correcting misspelled words shows only moderate improvements in the new version, it was already performing relatively well in this regard. Harnessing AI for Improved Accuracy.

Nonetheless, notable enhancements have been introduced. For instance, when Autocorrect alters a word you've typed, it will be highlighted with a yellow underline. Tapping on the word allows you to effortlessly revert to your original input.

Predictive Text

Enhancement with predictive text, iOS 17 introduces notable enhancements in Apple's intelligent input, particularly in the realm of predictive text. First and foremost, recommended text now appears at the end of the word you're currently typing, displayed in a lighter text format, as opposed to just appearing at the bottom of the screen. This adjustment significantly enhances the user experience.

Furthermore, iOS 17 offers phrase recommendations based on your frequently used phrases. Your iPhone or iPad learns these phrases over time, streamlining your texting process.

In a more permissive shift, Autocorrect has become less restrictive. Now, when you intend to express strong emotions, including expletives, your device won't attempt to substitute or censor them. This change marks a long-overdue evolution in autocorrect behavior.

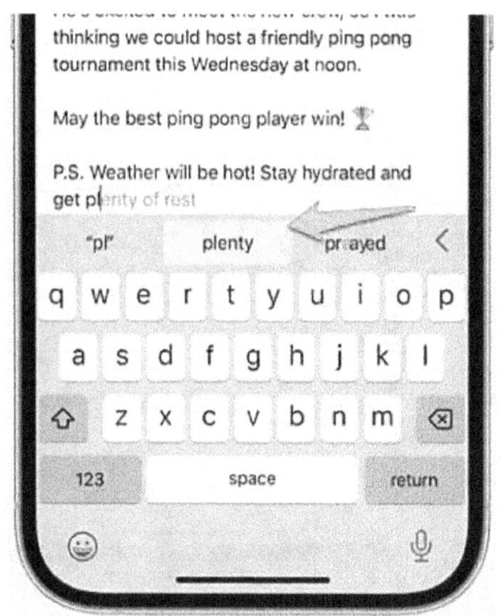

Autocorrect Functions As A Grammar Checker

The AI enhancements applied to Autocorrect in iOS 17 also cover grammar errors, which I find particularly beneficial.

Here's an example: In an email, if you write the sentence, "Will this affect your decision?" the word "affect" will be automatically highlighted in blue. Tapping on it will reveal the correct word for the sentence is "effect."

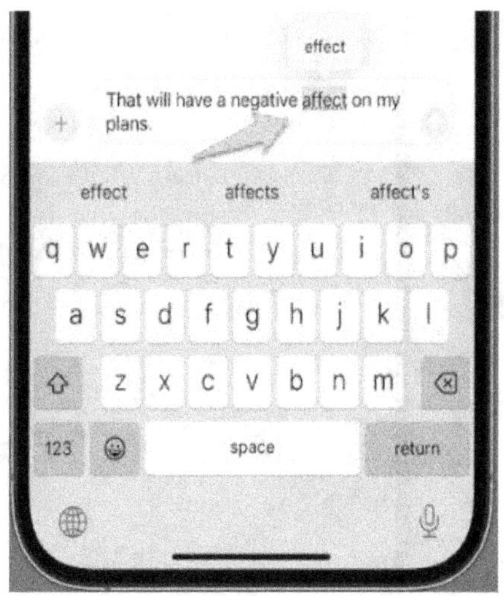

However, it's worth noting that these grammar suggestions don't appear until you've completed each sentence. You won't be alerted to potential grammar errors before that point.

You will not highlight or notify you of potential grammar errors as you type. Instead, it will only provide grammar suggestions or corrections after you have completed typing a sentence or phrase, making it impossible to catch or address grammar mistakes in real-time as you type.

Another integral aspect of the keyboard is Dictation, which now incorporates a state-of-the-art transformer-based speech recognition model, harnessing the power of the Neural Engine to enhance dictation accuracy significantly.

To evaluate this system, I used Dictation to transcribe a recording of Federighi's quote mentioned earlier into the text.
The results were only marginally satisfactory: Almost all the words were correct, but the word 'engine' was omitted entirely, and no punctuation was included, despite having the punctuation feature enabled.

Out of curiosity, I also had the new ChatGPT application perform the same transcription using OpenAI's Whisper. The app achieved 100% accuracy, including proper punctuation.

CHAPTER EIGHT

PRIVACY AND SECURITY UPGRADES

The iOS 17 features are designed to benefit a broader range of users. These features address various aspects of privacy, security, and convenience:

1. **Web Tracking Countermeasures:** The anti-web tracking measures, are aimed at preventing websites and online services from tracking your online behavior without your consent. This feature enhances user privacy by limiting the data collected by advertisers and other online entities.

2. **Safe Password Management**: The improved password management features allow users to securely store their passwords. This feature not only keeps your passwords safe but also simplifies the process of managing your login credentials for various accounts and services. It ensures that your sensitive information is protected from unauthorized access.

3. **Phishing-Resistant Passkeys**: This facilitates the sharing of phishing-resistant passkeys. These passkeys are a more secure way to authenticate and access your accounts, offering robust protection against phishing attempts, which are fraudulent efforts to obtain your sensitive information. This feature enhances security and safeguards users against common online threats.

In summary, these features contribute to a safer and more privacy-conscious digital experience by bolstering anti-tracking measures, providing secure password storage, and offering improved protection against phishing attacks. These enhancements benefit a wide user base, as they address critical aspects of online security and convenience.

Comprehensive Communication Safety

With the release of iOS 17 and iPadOS 17, Apple introduced Communication Safety, an optional or protective feature designed to notify children in case they receive or send photos containing nudity within the Messages app. When they are about to send or receive photos containing explicit content.

How does this work?

Once activated, the feature automatically blurs photos and videos containing nudity within compatible apps, while simultaneously alerting the child about the presence of sensitive content. Furthermore, this warning offers guidance on seeking assistance if needed. Apple is also introducing a new API, enabling developers to integrate Communication Safety support into their applications available on the App Store.

Communication Safety uses on-device processing to detect photos and videos containing nudity, ensuring that Apple and third parties cannot access the content, and that end-to-end encryption is preserved in the Messages app.

Communication Safety has been expanded to offer protections for sensitive videos and photos. This safeguard not only covers content exchanged through Messages but also includes data shared via AirDrop, the systemwide photo picker, FaceTime messages, Contact Posters within the Phone app, and even third-party applications.

Enabling Communication Safety on Your Kid's iPhone in iOS 17

Our smartphones have become an integral part of our lives, and when it comes to our children, they offer incredible opportunities for learning and connecting while also exposing them to potentially unsuitable content.

Enabling Communication Safety on your child's iPhone in iOS 17 is an essential step to protect them from potentially harmful content, such as explicit photos and videos. This feature extends its reach beyond iMessage, covering various communication methods.

Here's a detailed guide on how to enable Communication Safety:

1. Now, open the Settings app on your iPhone and navigate to 'Screen Time'.

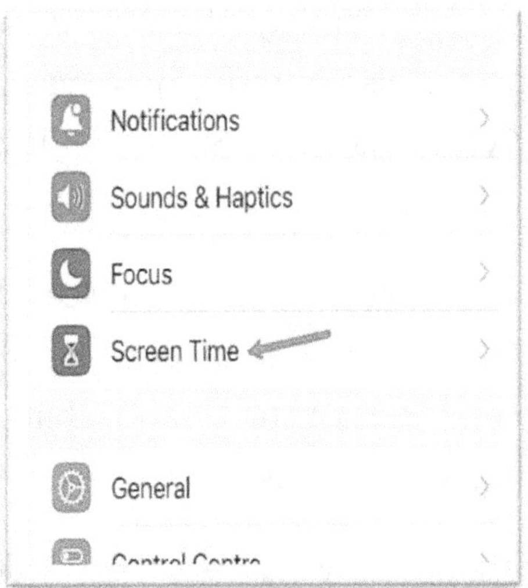

2. To enable the feature for a child within your family group, follow these steps:

- Tap the name of the child from your family group that you wish to enable the feature.
- Next, tap on the 'Communication Safety' option

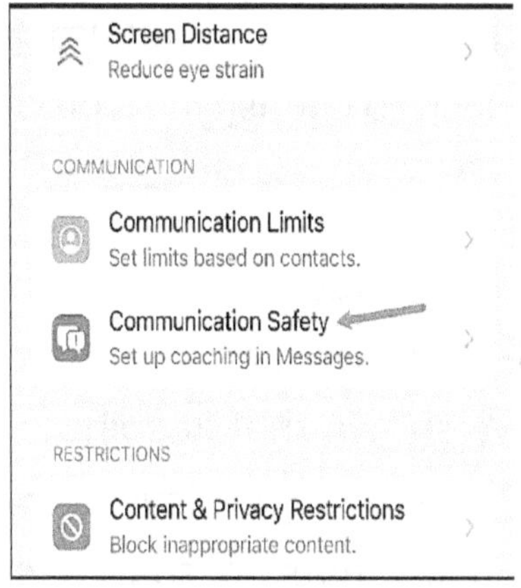

3. Hit 'Continue' to proceed.
   - Tap 'Continue' to move forward.
- Lastly, activate the switch for 'Check for Sensitive Photos'. You may be required to input the Screen Time passcode previously established for the child's device during the Screen Time setup.

CHAPTER NINE

OTHER ENHANCED FEATURES OF IOS17

Introducing a fresh application for writing and recollection, offering a novel approach to cherish life's precious moments and safeguard your memories.

Journal is a revolutionary app tailored for iPhone users, designed to foster self-reflection and gratitude through the art of journaling. Studies have shown that keeping a journal can significantly enhance well-being. Utilizing on-device machine learning, the app offers personalized prompts to spark inspiration for your journal entries. These prompts are intelligently drawn from your recent activities, encompassing photos, interactions, places visited, workouts, and more, streamlining the process of starting a journal entry. Scheduled notifications encourage you to cultivate a consistent journaling practice.

The journal places a strong emphasis on safeguarding your privacy. It features app locking, on-device data processing, and end-to-end encryption to ensure the utmost protection for your journal entries, with no access granted to anyone, including Apple.

Furthermore, with the introduction of the Journaling Suggestions API, developers can seamlessly integrate journaling prompts into their applications, expanding the reach of this transformative tool.

Advanced Camera Features:

iOS 17 introduces a comprehensive array of cutting-edge camera features, elevating the photography and videography experience on Apple devices.

- **Macro Photography:** With the new macro photography option, users can now capture intricate close-up shots with stunning detail and clarity. This feature is perfect for photographing small objects, and textures, or capturing the beauty of tiny details in the world around them.

- **Improved Night Mode:** The enhanced Night Mode takes low-light photography to the next level. It allows users to capture brighter, clearer, and more detailed photos in challenging lighting conditions, making it easier to take great shots in the dark or under dimly lit settings.

- **Video Editing Capabilities**: iOS 17 introduces new video editing capabilities that provide users with greater creative control over their videos. This allows for more intricate and polished video editing directly on their Apple devices, enabling users to refine their video content to their liking.

These camera enhancements not only improve the quality of photos and videos captured but also empower users to explore their creativity and storytelling abilities, making iOS 17 a significant upgrade for photography and videography enthusiasts.

Others also include:

Streamlined Password and Passkey Sharing

Sharing passwords is a breeze and more secure. Users can now share passwords with a group of trusted contacts, allowing everyone within the group to contribute and manage passwords, ensuring they stay up to date. The sharing takes place through iCloud Keychain, guaranteeing end-to-end encryption for added security.

Mental Health Features in the Health App

The Health app welcomes a range of new mental health features. Users can now log their daily moods and momentary emotions, identify potential contributing factors to their emotional well-being, and access assessments for depression and anxiety that are frequently employed in clinical settings. Furthermore, it introduces a unique feature designed to minimize the risk of myopia in children and reduce digital eyestrain for adults. The Screen Distance feature, utilizing the TrueDepth camera, encourages users to adjust their device's distance when held too close to their face for extended periods.

Offline Maps and Park Trail Discoveries in Maps

Maps get a substantial upgrade by introducing offline maps, enabling users to download specific areas and access turn-by-turn navigation, estimated arrival times, place discovery, and more, even when offline. Additionally, it simplifies the process of discovering thousands of trails in U.S. parks and provides real-time information on charging availability for electric vehicle drivers.

Expanded Sharing Capabilities for AirTag and Find My

AirTag now supports sharing with up to five other people, allowing friends and family to track items in Find My. In a shared group, all members can view the item's location, trigger a sound, and use Precision Finding to pinpoint the item's whereabouts. This feature extends to all other Find My Network accessories.

Collaborative Playlists and SharePlay in Apple Music

Apple Music welcomes Collaborative Playlists for a more collaborative music-listening experience. SharePlay in the car enables all passengers to contribute to the playlist, with each listener controlling the music from their own devices, regardless of whether they have an Apple Music subscription.

Enhanced AirPlay and Hotel TV Compatibility

Sharing content through AirPlay becomes more intuitive thanks to on-device learning of user preferences. AirPlay now extends its compatibility to supported hotel televisions, ensuring you can effortlessly enjoy your favorite content while traveling. This capability will be introduced in select hotels, starting with IHG Hotels & Resorts.

AirPods Unleash New Features

AirPods gain powerful new features, including Adaptive Audio, Personalized Volume, and Conversation Awareness, to redefine the personal audio experience. Enhanced Automatic Switching and call controls contribute to making AirPods even more user-friendly.

Comprehensive Activity History in the Home App

The Home app now offers users the ability to review up to 30 days of activity history for various devices, such as door locks, garage doors, alarm systems, and contact sensors. Additionally, two popular HomeKit lock features, tap to unlock and PIN codes, are now available for Matter-compatible locks.

Smart Grocery List in Reminders

Reminders now incorporate a smart grocery list feature that automatically categorizes added items, making shopping more efficient. Users can tailor how items are grouped, and the list remembers their preferences.

Visual Look Up in Videos and Photos

Visual Look Up has been expanded to paused video frames, allowing users to identify objects, storefronts, signs, and symbols, and extract subjects from photos and videos.

People Album Recognition in Photos

The People Album in Photos now employs on-device machine learning to identify more photos featuring your favorite people, along with cats and dogs.

Privacy Enhancements

In terms of privacy, Communication Safety extends beyond Messages, covering AirDrop, Contact Posters, FaceTime messages, and photo selection in the Photos app, now incorporating video content. A novel feature, Sensitive Content Warning, empowers adult users to steer clear of unwanted explicit images and videos. All image and video processing related to Sensitive Content Warning is exclusively performed on the device, ensuring Apple has no access to the content.

Empowering Accessibility Updates

Accessibility updates, including Assistive Access, which offers a customizable interface for users with cognitive disabilities. Live Speech enables nonspeaking users to type and have their words spoken during in-person or phone and FaceTime conversations. Personal Voice allows users at risk of speech loss to create a voice that closely resembles their own. Lastly, Point and Speak aids users who are blind or have low vision in reading text on physical objects by pointing. Etc.

CHAPTER TEN

EMBRACING iOS17

In our rapidly evolving digital landscape, remaining current with the latest technological innovations is imperative. For Apple enthusiasts and tech-savvy individuals alike, each iOS update is a highly anticipated event, and iOS 17 is certainly no different. Within this extensive guide, we will embark on a detailed exploration of iOS 17, uncovering its features, advantages, and compelling reasons that render it indispensable for Apple users.

This application is available for download to those who own newer iPhone models, and the phones compatible with this application include the iPhone XR, XS, XS Max, iPhone 11, iPhone SE (second generation and later), iPhone 12, iPhone 13, and iPhone 14, as indicated on Apple's website. It's worth noting that earlier iPhone models will not be compatible with this system update.

Exploring Further Possibilities

Regarding camera features, Apple could consider expanding its array of capture modes. Take, for instance, the Pixel 7, which offers the capability to create Photo Sphere images. While it might be seen as somewhat gimmicky, it empowers users to unleash their creativity, aligning with Apple's mission of pushing the boundaries of iPhone photography. Furthermore, the Pixel 7 boasts functionalities like Long Exposure and Action Pan for dynamic motion capture, which present opportunities for Apple to consider implementing in iOS 17.

Furthermore, this application introduces substantial enhancements to the Phone, Messages, and FaceTime applications, providing fresh avenues for self-expression in your communication. Additionally, the StandBy feature offers an all-new full-screen experience with easily accessible information designed to be viewed from a distance when you orient your iPhone on its side during the charging process.

Conclusion

This newest update blends innovation, enhanced efficiency, and a user-friendly interface, culminating in a transformative development. iOS 17 introduces significant enhancements to Phone, Messages, and FaceTime, offering novel means of self-expression in your communication. With StandBy, a fresh full-screen interface provides easily viewable information when you position your iPhone on its side during charging, allowing you to access at a glance from a distance.

The update brings and enhance the function ability and transformability of any iPhone supporting iOS17 with new security features and effective used and personalizing your phone.

INDEX